Fearless Presentations

By
Doug Staneart

Airleaf
Publishing

airleaf.com

ISBN: 1-59453-655-1

Contents

Why this Book was Written

When people find out that I teach public speaking classes, they often ask me if I could recommend a textbook on public speaking that is as simple and as easy to follow as my classes. Over the last ten years, I've recommended a number of different books, but I've had a difficult time finding a textbook that focused on public speaking in a step-by-step fashion and that anyone wanting to become a more confident speaker could easily follow. Don't get me wrong, I found many books that contained fabulous material about public speaking, but many of these books either reported everything under the sun about the topic—and so became very boring—or the information was presented in a very inefficient way.

So, this booklet is an attempt to present the basics of great speaking in a efficient and precise manner. I hope you enjoy the book and receive great benefit from it.

1. Public Speaking Anxiety

When I was in college, I had an internship with a large oil and gas company. While I was working there, I felt like I really impressed the people around me with my work ethic, determination, resourcefulness, and productivity. Many of the projects that I worked on were finished weeks and even months ahead of schedule to everyone's surprise.

But at the end of the internship, I, along with a half-dozen other interns, was asked to give a presentation to the executive committee who created the intern program. Of course my boss was in this meeting...and my boss's boss...and three vice-presidents, all of my intern peers, and various observers.

In the beginning, I didn't think much of this presentation, but as the day moved closer and closer, I began to get more and more nervous. I was the youngest person ever to be accepted to this program— just 19 years old. The next youngest intern was 23 and was in her second year of law school. So, I felt a little out-classed to say the least.

My boss told me that this would be a great opportunity to shine. He said that if I could just get across to this group how productive I had been to the company, then I would have no problem getting a generous permanent offer from the company upon graduation. *That just made me even more nervous.*

I wrote, memorized, and practiced my speech over and over. I had a flawless delivery. I realized that I needed a few visuals, so I created a couple of black and white cutouts of topics I'd be covering.

The big day came, and as I walked into the room, trembling from the fear and pressure, I noticed that every single person had on a nicely pressed suit. I was wearing slacks with a shirt and tie, but no jacket. *I didn't even own a jacket.* The pressure began to build even more.

As the first presenter was introduced, she walked to the front of the room, sat down a manila folder, turned on her overhead projector (this was in the days before PowerPoint,) and put up a beautiful, color-filled slide. *Why in the world had I not thought of using an overhead!* My palms began to sweat profusely.

When the second presenter began to speak, I became even more nervous. He had the audience laughing and nodding their heads within minutes, and created a true rapport with the audience. *I didn't have any jokes in my presentation, and I couldn't see how anyone would be nodding in agreement with me, because I was just prepared to recite some facts.* My stomach churned.

It was now my turn. As the director called my name, I stood and moved my hands to pick up my notes. When I did, the napkin that my hand was resting on came with me—attached as a result of the sweat that now seemed to be pouring from my palms. As I peeled it off, I picked up my notes, and I could see the pages shaking in my hand. I just prayed that the people in the audience couldn't see it.

As I spoke my first sentence, I could feel the beads of sweat on my forehead, so I pulled the sleeve of my white shirt across my brow. A few seconds later I used the other sleeve and continued alternating them throughout the presentation.

I talk pretty fast anyway, but when I get nervous, ITalkRealFast!SoFastThatItWouldMakeYourEyeballsS pin! I gave my entire 15-minute speech in less than five minutes and said every word.

As I looked into the faces in the audience, no one was nodding. Most people just had blank looks of confusion. When I sat down, there was utter silence in the room. The director called a break. I looked at my sleeves, and they were soaked to my skin. I was so embarrassed that I wanted to crawl under the table and die. If I could have walked out of that room and never laid eyes on any of those people again, I would have gladly done so.

About seven months later, when the intern committee from this company came back to my school, my adviser pulled me aside and told me that they had told him that they would not be extending an offer to have me back. I was crushed. I had never failed this badly at anything.

I tell you that story so you can see that if I can become a good enough speaker that people actually pay me to speak...then ANYONE can do this!

As a result of that failure, for next few years, when I had opportunities to present to a group, I began to either defer to someone else, or make excuses to get out of speaking. During that time, I learned a valuable lesson:

———————————————

Right or wrong, people form a perception about our competence based on how confidently we present ourselves.

———————————————

Let me give you an example.

Let's say you have a pain in your side and you go see a doctor about it. The doctor looks at you and says, "Uhm...Well, uh you know? You might, uhm, have to have your uh appendix taken out." How competent are you going to feel about this doctor's ability to treat you? Or even worse—the doctor says all the right things, but as he looks over your chart, you notice his hand shaking. It doesn't matter how many degrees this person has or how many initials the doctor has after his or her name. You will probably question the doctor's competence.

That is exactly what happened to me during that first presentation. I realized that even though I had been a respected and valued employee of the company, the negative perception that was formed about me during my presentation counteracted all of the goodwill I had previously developed. I vowed that the same thing would never happen to me again. I was going to do whatever I had to do to make sure that the next time I gave a presentation, I would give the audience a true representation of my abilities.

The problem I had was that I didn't know where to start. Where do you go to become a better speaker? The first thing I did was join a Toastmasters group. The people who attended the club that I joined were fantastic people. I still consider many of them friends today. But as I watched each present, I noticed even the most senior members were not the captivating speakers that I wanted to become. In fact, most of the talks I heard were not very compelling. Most were down-right boring. I began to ask some of the members how long it had taken them to get to the level they were at in the group, and the first I talked to said, "15 years." I was shocked. First, I knew I didn't want to spend the next 15 years struggling with this. And besides, after 15 years of practice, this guy still wasn't a great speaker.

It reminded me of when I first took up golf. I didn't have a lot of money, so I bought a cheap set of clubs and went out to the driving range. I hacked around for a few weeks, but I seemed to be getting worse than when I first started. The golf pro from the pro-shop saw me struggling and asked if I wanted to take a few lessons. I told him I had more time than money, so I'd just keep practicing on my own for a while. I said, "You know what they say, practice make perfect."

He smiled and replied, "They are wrong. Practice does not make perfect. Practice makes permanent. If you practice a bad golf swing over and over, then you're just going to get really good at a bad golf swing. And when you come to me later, it's just going to take that much longer to break your old habits."

That's exactly what my friends in the toasting club had been doing all those years. I realized that if I really wanted to be a great speaker, that I was going to have to learn from great speakers. So I got a coach—one that actually made a living speaking in front of groups.

Since that day, I have attended over a dozen different public speaking classes, trained with some of the most highly paid public speaking coaches in the world, and taught over 600 public speaking modules, and in that time, I have identified a number of simple, key things that anyone can do to overcome fear and nervousness in front of a group. I have used these things myself with great success. Over the last ten years in my public speaking classes, I've watched the confidence of thousands of people grow and develop in a matter of minutes as a result of using these few simple techniques.

On the following pages, you will find an outline of tips and techniques that successful speakers have used for centuries to create solid, polished first impressions and deliver dynamic, fearless presentations.

Universal Fear

A number of years ago in an episode of Seinfeld, Jerry Seinfeld talked about a poll that had been conducted in which Americans said that their number one fear was public speaking, and that the fear of death was number five. He said, "...that would mean that at a funeral, people are five times more likely to want to be in the casket than giving the eulogy. "Some of the best humor usually has an element of truth in it. What we can learn from this is that when we feel nervous in front of a group—we're normal! Almost everyone feels that nervousness and anxiety. The very best speakers are the ones that put that fear aside and perform anyway.

Below are a few simple things you can do to help you perform better in your next presentation and ease some of your nervousness and anxiety.

1. **Realize 90% of Nervousness doesn't Show:** Most of the symptoms of nervousness—butterflies, sweaty palms, faster heartbeat, etc.—never show to an audience. If you set your notes down on a lectern, the audience won't even be able to see shaky hands.

2. **Written Material:** Never, never, never, never, never write out a talk word for word unless absolute accuracy must be maintained as in legal situations. Otherwise, just make brief notes. A little spontaneity adds a tremendous amount of character to your talk. Written speeches are almost always boring, and when you read text, it is much more difficult to make a connection with your audience.

3. **Committing Your Talk to Memory:** Never memorize a talk word for word. Memorizing a talk word for word can actually lead to more anxiety. If something out of the ordinary happens or if you ever lose your place, you will put an extreme amount of pressure on yourself to get back. A better way to memorize a talk is to narrow your talk down to just a few main ideas and commit those main ideas to memory. If during your presentation you have additional time, you can add additional details to the main ideas, and if time runs short

(which it often does,) you can rest assured that your main points were delivered.

4. **Show up Early:** Get an idea for the setting, mingle with your audience, and test any equipment that you will be using.

5. **Take a Few Deep Breaths:** When many of us get nervous, we tend to take shallow breaths. This robs our brain of oxygen and can create a negative reinforcing cycle. What happens is that we originally take a shallow breath out of nervousness and try to speak. Somewhere along the way, we realize that we won't be able to finish our sentence, so we speed up. That makes us more nervous, and our next breath is even more shallow. When this cycle occurs, just pause, take a deep breath, and continue.

6. **Look for a Friendly Face:** As you are approaching the front, make eye-contact with a few friendly faces in the audience. Smile, and they will probably smile back. It will put you both at ease.

7. **Drop your Hands:** Your hands and your gestures can add great impact to your delivery, but when you are not using your hands, just drop them to your side. It will feel awkward at first, but dropping your hands to your side is the most natural gesture you can use. For instance, when you walk down the hallway at your office, do you cup your hands in

front as you walk? Is it more natural to lock your hands behind you when you walk? Probably not. In most situations, it is natural to just let your hands drop to your side. When you do this, it will allow you to make more purposeful gestures when you need to. (See Chapter 6 on Gestures and Movement.)

8. **Speak Only on Topics on which You are an Expert:** One of the reasons that speech classes and toasting clubs can actually make people more nervous is that the topics we choose to present on during these activities are topics that we put together after just a little research. If someone is going to ask you to present about a business topic, the main reason would be because you are the most qualified person to speak on the topic. You are qualified because of your experience. Your delivery should be as casual as if your best friend came up to you and asked, "How's your project going?" This will allow you to deliver your topic is a way that makes the audience feel as if you are talking to each person directly.

9. **Be Excited about Your Topic:** If you aren't excited or enthused about your topic, then no one else will be either. If you give your audience energy, they will give energy back to you.

10. **Practice:** Rather than practicing your presentation in front of a mirror (when we do this, we tend to

find things to nitpick that an audience would never notice,) try practicing your delivery by using it in a conversation with a friend or loved one. "Hey, have I told you about the project I'm working on…"

After training thousands of people to become better speakers, one thing that I know for sure is that EVERYONE gets nervous when they present. Exceptional speakers just don't show it. In fact, in many cases, the great speaker will use that nervousness to his or her advantage. The next chapter will show you how.

ACTION ITEM

Make a list of things that happen to your body when you get nervous speaking to groups (butterflies in the stomach, sweaty palms, etc.)

1. _____
2. _____
3. _____
4. _____
5. _____

Which of these things will an audience actually be able to see?

Which of the 10 tips will help you reduce each of the items you listed above?

2. The Secret of Great Presentations

If you take only one piece of advice from this book, make sure that it is the pearl of wisdom in this chapter. If you focus on this one simple thing, the number of times you say "uhm" won't matter. If you focus on this one thing, your gestures and not knowing what to do with your hands won't matter. If you focus on this one thing, then the occasional loss of train of thought won't matter. In fact, if you focus on this one simple thing, you can break just about every rule that public speakers are supposed to abide by, and you will still win over your audience.

This one simple rule has transformed countless mediocre speakers into good speakers, scores of good speakers into great speakers, and numerous great speakers into world-class speakers.

This simple rule that can make or break a speaker is …enthusiasm.

That's right, if you have a little excitement in your talk and a spring in your step, people pay attention. Your audience will have just about as much excitement about your talk as you do, and no more. So, if you want to win over your audience, add a sparkle of enthusiasm.

One of my mentors gave me two rules to live by in the world of professional speakers. She said, "Rule number one is to never speak on a topic that you yourself are not enthusiastic about, and rule number two is that if you ever violate rule number one, fake it 'til you make it." Frank Bettger in his book *How I Raised Myself from Failure to Success in Selling* said it a different way. He said, "If you act enthusiastic, then you'll be enthusiastic."

For those of us who get nervous in front of groups, it's even easier. In the previous chapter I pointed out that 90% of our nervousness doesn't even show. Let's look at the other 10%. When we are nervous, we often cut out preambles and get right to the point, our rate of speech typically speeds up, we tend to move around a lot more, and we may move our hands around more than normal. Well, when we are excited about something, we do the exact same things.

Years ago, when I was a sales manager, I was often amazed at the number of times that a brand new sales person without a lot of product knowledge and absolutely no experience, could close sale after sale while my more seasoned people were struggling. The more times I went on sales calls with these new people, the more I started to notice a pattern. New salespeople are often nervous, so when they walk into an office on a sales call, they tend to cut right to the chase. They also generally talk faster because they are afraid they'll forget something. They have a tough time sitting still because of the nervousness, so they move around a lot.

I noticed that these symptoms of nervousness worked to the advantage of these new salespeople, because their prospects looked across the table at salespeople who appeared to be extremely enthusiastic about what they were selling. I would imagine that these potential buyers were saying things to themselves like, "if this person believes so much in this product, it must be good," and then they'd buy the product.

We as speakers can also use our nervousness to our advantage. When we turn that pent up nervousness into energy and enthusiasm, our audience can't help but be energized as well. So the next time you are asked to speak to a group, instead of focusing on the nervousness, focus on your energy. If you have to fake it at first, don't worry, because the energy you give to your audience will be returned to you. When your audience begins to have fun, you will too.

Just like Frank Bettger said, "If you act enthusiastic, then you'll be enthusiastic."

ACTION ITEM

List three things you can do during your next presentation to help you look and act more enthusiastic?

1. _____
2. _____
3. _____

3. Introductions and Conclusions

In our technology centered world, information moves very quickly. We are constantly bombarded with so much information that out of necessity, we disregard much of what we are exposed to. Psychologists fifty years ago determined that the average attention span of a person is just two-minutes. Today, they say that the average attention span is just eight seconds. If you doubt their findings, listen to a headline news report on the radio or TV. Most of the news stories will be less than eight seconds in length, and those that are longer will often be broken up by sound bites that are, you guessed it, about eight seconds long.

My point is that if we want to gain and keep the attention of our audience, we only have a few seconds to do it. So rather than starting with a preamble such as, "My talk is about," or "I'm going to tell you about," just jump right in. Get their attention like a newspaper story or TV reporter would by giving the **who, what, when, and where** in the first couple of sentences.

If you are beginning with a story about a personal experience, then you might start with a sentence such as, "About **two years ago**, **I** was working on a similar project with **Joe and Steve** in **Dallas**..." That type of beginning gets people's attention.

The "Who, What, When, Where" is a fast and easy way to get your audience's attention quickly and get the specifics of your talk out to your audience in a clear and concise manner. This type of introduction works extremely well, especially if you begin your speech with an anecdote or a personal story.

Another way of getting attention quickly is to start at the most impactful part of your report. Movie makers have learned this lesson. If you watch a classic film, it will probably follow a timeline where there is an introduction that slowly builds to a climax and then the movie ends in a conclusion that ties everything up in a nice little bow.

Movies today don't have that luxury. If some type of action isn't happening in the first few minutes, many moviegoers may get up to leave. Movies today start with a lot of action, controversy, or suspense to capture our attention, and then fill in the details of previous events later as flashbacks if needed.

We can use this same technique in our talks as well. We can start at the most impactful part of our report, and then fill in details later as we need to. For example, if we are leading a safety meeting, we might start with an opening like, "32 people lost a limb, 12 people were decapitated, and eight people died last year because they forgot to do one simple thing." Or if we are giving a financial report, we might begin with, "We were

$32,000 under budget this quarter and this is how we did it."

Conclusions

One thing that we have to remember as speakers is that we communicate in words, but our minds think in pictures. Therefore, even with as complicated and complex a machine as the human brain is, when we communicate, we need to focus on one specific point at a time.

Let me give you an example. Think about an elephant. What do you see in your mind? You have probably formed a picture in your mind of an elephant. You can see the trunk, the big ears, the leathery skin. Now think of the Statue of Liberty. What do you see in your mind now? Do you see the statue? Can you see the torch and the green discoloration of the copper? The big question, however, is where did the elephant go? Your picture of the Statue of Liberty probably replaced the picture of the elephant. When we know that this is how our mind works, then we can use it to our advantage when we speak.

Rather than having ten main points or twenty main points, our maximum number should be five. In most cases, three is a better number, and for short talks, we should have no more than one main point. The bulk of your talk should be built around supporting each of these main points.

The reason we want to limit our main points is simple. An old Chinese proverb says, "Man who chase after two rabbits catch none." It's the same with speaking. If we cover ten different items in a cursory fashion, our audience is likely to remember none of them. But if we focus on one main item and support our idea with evidence, our audience is more likely to retain the information.

"But aren't there times when we need to cover more key points?" I'm sure that there are certain times where the above guideline doesn't fit, but they are rare.

I've had people ask me, "Sure, that sounds good, but what about on a bid presentation? We need to get across to the audience that we are good at quality, timeliness, staying under budget, safety, experience, teamwork, and a myriad of other things. How do we get all of that across in three main points?" My answer is always the same..."You don't. Out of all of those things that you mentioned, one is definitely going to be the most important to the decision-makers. If you can find out what area of interest that is, and you build your presentation around it, you have almost a 100% chance of getting the job, because your competition is likely to have a watered down presentation covering everything."

My advice is always to ask questions of the decision-makers before creating your presentation to find out which of the areas that you *could* focus on would be the **ONE** most important to these decision-makers. The bulk of your presentation should be focused on this one thing. Then, find out what is second-most-important and give that point a little less time. Do the same with the third-most-important. (It's best to focus on three just in case the thing we have determined is most important turns out not to be.) If you can prove to the group beyond a shadow of a doubt that you are capable of accomplishing the top three things that are most important to these decision makers (and your competition doesn't) you have a very good shot at winning the bid.

This technique can be used with any presentation. If you start by designing your talk focusing on the number one most important thing to your audience, then the people listening to your talk will be all ears. You'll be telling them exactly what they want to hear and what they need to hear.

"What about meetings? We always have a minimum of ten things we have to cover in our meetings." This is going to seem harsh, but if you are trying to cover that many topics in your meetings, then your meetings are probably **VERY** long and boring, and your meetings probably don't accomplish much. Narrow the agenda down and see if you get better results. If you don't, then go back to the way you were doing them before.

Whether you are in a meeting, or any presentation really, the whole reason for narrowing your points down to just a few main topics, is that this process makes the conclusion so much easier. If you have narrowed your topic down to three key points, then your conclusion could be as simple as a summary. "So in summary, my three main points are 1, 2, and 3." By doing your conclusion this way, you are refreshing the memory of your audience as well as tying a nice bow around the information you just presented to them.

Another option for your conclusion would be to ask your audience to take some type of action especially if you are trying to persuade your audience. Of course when you ask them to take this action, it's always a good idea to let them know how they will benefit from doing what you ask.

An example of this type of conclusion would be, "Based on what we've just covered, I'd ask you to..., and if you do that, then you will get..." More on this in Chapter Five: *Being Persuasive*.

Whichever way you decide to conclude, prepare your final words in advance and be clear and concise. Limit your conclusion to just a couple of sentences and you will have great success.

4. The Power of Stories

When I was about six-years-old, I stole a dollar from my dad's nightstand. When he found out what I had done, he sat me down and told me a story about how when he was a young man, he and an army buddy were a little short on cash, so before they went on a weekend leave, they borrowed (stole) about $0.25 worth of gasoline from the base pumps and headed into town. The MP's caught up with them before they got off the base and if it hadn't been for a very understanding commanding officer, he and his buddy would still be serving time in a military stockade. He said that according to the army, the value of the theft doesn't matter, it is the action itself that created the consequences.

Throughout my lifetime, my dad has offered me countless pieces of advice, but it would be very difficult for me to try to remember specific individual lessons that he taught me. But I do remember that story. Telling a personal story is a great way to capture the attention of your audience, and stories have a magical longevity that sticks with people much longer than a lecture or an order.

In an article in <u>Training and Development Magazine</u> titled *Leadership Through Storytelling*, the author tells us that "People like to hear stories and they tend to repeat them.

"In business as well as in other settings, storytelling works as a useful technique to

- "Capture people's attention
- Send a message people will remember
- Establish rapport
- Build credibility
- Bring a team closer together"

Our audience relates to storytelling because when we hear a story, we tend to relate the story to something from our own personal experience. For instance, if I told you about a friend of mine who was killed in a drunk driving accident, your subconscious mind tries to relate the story to a personal experience of your own. So you may subconsciously search through stored memories to find a similar incident from your own life. You might remember a time when you had a little too much to drink, a time when someone you knew had a little too much to drink and got behind the wheel, or you might remember a time when you saw a film in high school about drunk driving. The storytelling process builds credibility with your audience because your audience's own memories verify the truth of the original story. By doing this, the story helps build rapport between you and your audience like magic.

If you want to dazzle your audience, tell more personal stories.

So how to we find suitable personal stories? All we have to do is ask ourselves a series of questions such as, "When did I first realize that the point that I am trying to make in my talk was valid?" or "When was the last time I took this advice myself?"

Stories can be very powerful in persuading your audience as well. In the next chapter, we'll use personal stories to help us change the opinion or behavior of others without raising resentment.

ACTION ITEM

Catalogue stories of experiences you have had that others can learn from.

1) Create a list of successes you've had in business—a promotion you received, an idea your company adopted, a project that was finished early or under budget, a time you dealt effectively with a tough customer, etc.

_____

_____

_____

_____

2) Create a list of challenges or set backs that you might have had in your career.

_____

_____

_____

_____

3) Create a list of mistakes that you have made in your life that were learning experiences.

_____

_____

_____

_____

4) Create of list of meaningful "firsts" in your life. For example, first job, first date, first child, first speeding ticket, etc.

_____

_____

_____

_____

5) Make a list of key tasks or steps in doing your job, then go back to each task and think of a story of some time when you realized that doing these tasks well would lead to success in your career.

_____

_____

_____

_____

5. Being Persuasive

"**Four score and seven years ago our fathers brought forth on this continent a new nation** conceived in liberty and dedicated to the proposition that all men are created equal. Now we are engaged in a great civil war, testing whether that nation or any nation so conceived and so dedicated can long endure.

"We are met on a great battlefield of that war. We have come to dedicate a portion of that field as a final resting-place for those who here gave their lives that that nation might live. It is altogether fitting and proper that we should do this. But in a larger sense, we cannot dedicate, we cannot consecrate, we cannot hallow this ground. The brave men, living and dead who struggled here have consecrated it far above our poor power to add or detract. The world will little note nor long remember what we say here, but it can never forget what they did here.

"It is for us the living rather to be dedicated here to the unfinished work which they who fought here have thus far so nobly advanced. It is rather for us to be here dedicated to the great task remaining before us—**that from these honored dead we take increased devotion** to that cause for which they gave the last full measure of devotion—that we here highly resolve that these dead shall not have died in vain, **that this nation under God shall have a new birth of freedom**, and that government of the people, by the people, for the people shall not perish from the earth."

The Gettysburg Address is arguably Abraham Lincoln's most famous and most quoted speech. His purpose was two-fold. First, to honor the fallen soldiers who sacrificed their lives on the battlefield, and second, to persuade a divided nation to mend fences. Most amazing of all though is that he did it in less than a minute and a half.

In the Bible, Luke 13:4-5, Jesus says, "**Or those eighteen, upon whom the tower in Siloam fell**, and slew them, think ye that they were sinners above all men that dwelt in Jerusalem? **I tell you, nay: but, except ye repent, ye shall all likewise perish.**"

To his Jewish listeners, the story of Siloam was a well-known part of their history. To his listeners, he was very persuasive in just about ten seconds.

Here is a more recent example: President George W. Bush in 2002 said, "For many Americans, these four months have brought sorrow, and pain that will never completely go away. **Every day a retired firefighter returns to Ground Zero, to feel closer to his two sons who died there.** At a memorial in New York, a little boy left his football with a note for his lost father: Dear Daddy, please take this to heaven. I don't want to play football until I can play with you again some day.

"Our enemies send other people's children on missions of suicide and murder. They embrace tyranny and death as a cause and a creed. We stand for a different choice, made long ago, on the day of our founding. We affirm it again today. **We choose freedom and the dignity of every life.** Steadfast in our purpose, we now press on. We have known freedom's price. We have shown freedom's power. **And in this great conflict, my fellow Americans, we will see freedom's victory."**

All of these examples share a common process to persuade the audience. Each example starts off will the Who, What, When, Where:

- "Four score and seven years ago our fathers brought forth on this continent a new nation..."
- "Or those eighteen, upon whom the tower in Siloam fell, and slew them..."
- "Every day a retired firefighter returns to Ground Zero, to feel closer to his two sons who died there."

Each speaker also tells a story as an example of the point he is trying to convey, and then tells the audience what action he wants the audience to take:

- "...that from these honored dead we take increased devotion..."
- "Nay: but, except ye repent..."

- "We choose freedom and the dignity of every life."

And finally, each ends with the benefit that the **audience will receive** if they do what the speaker suggests:

- "that this nation under God shall have a new birth of freedom, and that government of the people, by the people, for the people shall not perish from the earth."
- "...but, except ye repent, ye shall all likewise perish."
- "And in this great conflict, my fellow Americans, we will see freedom's victory."

This simple formula is one of the most effective ways that we have found to persuade people. Or if tension is high and trust between the parties is not strong, even if we don't persuade the other party, we might at least allow ourselves *to be heard* by the other party. The three-step process is the **IAB formula**.

I-Incident or Story: Tell a story to establish rapport, gain credibility, and build common ground with your audience. Personal incidents tend to work best in these situations.

A-Action: Tell your audience what exactly you want them to do based on the story that you just relayed to them. This action statement should be crisp and concise. The fewer words the better.

B-Benefit to the Audience: Tell the audience what they will get if they do what you ask. This should also be very clear and concise, and should be totally focused on the benefit that the **audience** will receive.

Here's an example. Let's say you have an employee, a sales representative, who has a habit of showing up late for work. A personal example like this might work to help persuade him to come in earlier.

"**When I first started in sales about ten years ago, I was so excited about my new job, that I used to come in to the office about an hour before everyone else** just to make sure I was prepared to start the day. One of these mornings the phone rang at 7:29 in the morning, and since I was the only one there, I answered it. A man named Bill Lawley who was the president of a major commercial real estate company asked me to drop by to talk to him about doing some work for his people. By 9:00 that morning, I had closed a $13,000 piece of business, and in the next four weeks, I closed three more just like it. I found out that the decision-makers like to work early in the morning, and they like to do business with people who work early in the morning as well. **You should try coming in early** and if you do, **you'll see that your income will go up dramatically.**"

Your audience is more likely to remember the story than they would an order that you give them, and they will be much more likely to cooperate enthusiastically. People don't like to be dictated to or ordered, but many will gladly do things that you suggest indirectly if it is clearly in their best interest. By telling them exactly what you want them to do, you avoid miscommunication, and by telling them how they will benefit from the action that you suggest, you are motivating them more effectively as well.

So if you want to get more enthusiastic cooperation from your audience, try using the IAB formula.

(I) Incident
(A) Action
(B) Benefit

ACTION ITEM

Take a few of the story ideas you came up with in the Chapter 4 Action Item step and add in an Action and a Benefit for each.

(I) Incident _____
_____
_____

(A) Action _____

_____

(B) Benefit _____

_____

(I) Incident _____

_____

_____

(A) Action _____

_____

(B) Benefit _____

_____

(I) Incident _____

_____

_____

(A) Action _____

_____

_____

(B) Benefit _____

_____

_____

(I) Incident _____
_____
_____

(A) Action _____
_____

(B) Benefit _____
_____

6. Gestures & Movement

The best rule of thumb for gestures and movement while public speaking is simple—move when you need to.

When I first began speaking, I was always concerned with trivial things such as *what should I do with my hands? Should I scan the audience with my eyes, or look over everyone's head? How do I keep from fidgeting?*

Because I focused on those trivial things, my message was lost in a lot of minutia. I was more focused on myself and less focused on the message that I was trying to deliver. Consequently, I distracted myself, I lost my place and made myself more nervous, which caused me to fidget, avoid eye contact with my audience, and worry more about my hands. It was a reinforcing downward spiral.

However, once I began doing the few things we've covered in the first few chapters—being enthusiastic about my topic, telling more stories, using the IAB formula—my focus shifted off of myself and onto my message. Many of the nervous habits went away automatically without me having to do anything at all.

However, there are a few things that we can consciously do to make ourselves appear more poised in front of a group. Keep in mind, that as you become more confident in front of a group and more self-assured when you speak, many of these things will happen automatically. So, don't spend a lot of time thinking about these things in the beginning. As you become more and more confident, if you find that some of these things are still distracting you, then focus on improving one area at a time.

First Impressions

Realize that the first impression that your audience has of you often is created before you take the stage. The way you carry yourself, your posture, and your conversations with audience members can all have a part in creating your first impression. So, as you walk to the front of the room, make sure your chin is up, make eye contact with a few friendly faces, smile, and have some enthusiasm in your step. An easy way to harness enthusiasm is to just walk about a stride or so faster than your normal pace.

This one simple thing can have a profound effect. What is your automatic impression if the speaker slowly walks to the front with little or no enthusiasm. Chances are you will begin to think that this meeting is going to be dull. Even before the speaker opens his or her mouth.

Once you take the stage, make sure to distribute your weight evenly on both feet. The reason is that if your weight is centered on one foot, eventually, it will tire, you will want to shift to the other foot, and before long, you will constantly be shifting from one foot to the other. There is nothing inherently wrong with that, but it might eventually become a distraction to your audience, and anything that distracts from your message can have a negative impact on your performance.

If you've ever wondered, "What do I do with my hands?," don't worry, that is a natural question that almost everyone has. The answer is to drop your hands to your side when you are not using them. It will feel unnatural at first, but you'll find the results quite rewarding. If you clasp your hands in front of you, then when you need to use them, you have to first let go, and then use them. And your subconscious mind would rather just keep them clasped. Therefore, we miss opportunities to make natural gestures. If you were in the military, you are probably more likely to rest your hands behind you. This can be negative for the same reason, but can be doubly distracting because people in the audience after a while will begin to wonder, "What is the speaker doing behind his/her back?" You'll find that when you drop your hands to your side, you will be much more natural at using them to dramatize your speech when you need to.

What about eye contact? Make eye contact with friendly faces in the audience. This will help the audience members feel that you are speaking to them directly instead of lecturing to them. It will also help you build confidence, because these people will give you subtle positive reinforcement like nods and smiles.

Move around as much as you need to when it is appropriate. But always remember to avoid repetitive patterns. Anything you do too much can be a distraction.

There is very little difference between movements and gesture that you would do when you speak to someone in a one-on-one situation and the gestures you might use in front of a group. The only major exception to this rule is that as your audience gets bigger, so should your gestures. You may have to exaggerate your gestures if you are speaking to a coliseum, but in most cases, do what comes naturally.

ACTION ITEM

When introduced, throw your shoulders back, stand with confidence, and move to the front about a half-step faster to generate more enthusiasm.

7. The Talk to Inform

Sometimes, we just need to get information across to our audience in a poised and confident way. The Three-Point Talk format is a simple way to do this.

To deliver a great Three-Point Talk, you just have to remember three basic steps.

1. Limit your topic to the three most important points.
2. Develop compelling support for each point.
3. Summarize the points to conclude.

Limit your Topic to Three Main Points

Remember, the human mind can only totally focus on one thing at a time. So, unless you can hone your talk into three points or less, your audience will have a tough time retaining your information. It's okay to give additional information, but the more information outside of the scope of the three main points, the more diluted your entire message will be.

This Three-Point process also helps us as speakers create a clear and concise message for our audience. As we become more clear in our delivery, our audience becomes more clear about our topic as well. It is easy for the audience to follow our train of thought, and easier for them to stay focused on our topic.

Develop Compelling Support for each Point

The second major key to a successful Three-Point talk is to offer your audience some support to back up your three key points. Real-life examples, statistics, expert opinions, and other support material can add additional credibility to your message.

The personal stories that we have talked about in the last several chapters are excellent real-life examples that can be quite compelling. Everyone loves a story.

Statistics can also be effective, but be careful. Dale Carnegie, in his book *The Quick and Easy Way to Effective Speaking*, said, "Statistics of themselves are boring. They should be judiciously used and should be clothed in language that makes them vivid and graphic."

The testimony of an expert can also add a great deal of credibility to your message. According to Cordell & Cordell, PC, "as many as 50% of all court cases utilize an expert in some capacity. Furthermore, surveys of judges have demonstrated that judges regard expert testimony as very influential in their ultimate decision, particularly where the court appoints the expert." If this type of support can influence a judge, it might be a great way to influence the people we are speaking to as well.

Summarize

Finally, to ensure that our main points are remembered, it might be a good idea to end with a summary. The best and easiest way to end a three-point talk is to just list the three key points one more time to refresh the memory of your audience.

So in summary, the three main steps to giving a great talk to inform are first, to…

1. Limit your topic to three main points
2. Develop compelling support for each topic, and
3. Summarize your main points in conclusion.

ACTION ITEM

Use this structure to design your next talk. Keep your main points to three or less, and your audience will enjoy your presentation more and retain the information you deliver better.

Topic: _____

Point #1: _____

Compelling Support A: _____

Compelling Support B: _____

Point #2: _____

Compelling Support A: _____

Compelling Support B: _____

Point #3: _____

Compelling Support A: _____

Compelling Support B: _____

8. Add more Impact to your Presentation

After the basic structure of your three-point talk is created, you can add additional zing to your talk by adding analogies, demonstrations, samples, anecdotes, or other pieces of showmanship. Since the previous chapter actually used the structure of the three-point talk to explain the three-point talk, let's add a few of these impact ideas to the previous chapter to see if we can make it even more relatable and compelling.

* * * * * * *

To deliver a great Three-Point Talk, you just have to remember three basic steps.

1. Limit your topic to the three most important points.
2. Develop compelling support for each point.
3. Summarize the points to conclude.

Limit your Topic to Three Main Points

Remember, the human mind can only totally focus on one thing at a time. So, unless you can hone your talk into three points or less, your audience will have a tough time retaining your information. (Analogy) *It is similar to driving down a busy highway. So much information is all around us, that it would be very difficult to store and memorize everything we see. But if someone gave us some simple directions with a few landmarks, those specific landmarks are easier to spot. By giving a brief introduction of what the three main points are, we are telling our audience what landmarks to pay attention to.*

It's okay to give additional information, but the more information outside of the scope of the three main points, the more diluted the message will be.

This three-point process also helps us as speakers create a clear and concise message for our audience. As we become more clear in our delivery, our audience becomes more clear about our topic as well. It is easy for the audience to follow our train of thought, and easier for them to stay focused on our topic. (Personal Example) *In fact, three months ago, I had a company approach me to put together a program to help their executives and managers measure the work of their employees in order to develop their direct reports. In the beginning, I felt a little overwhelmed asking myself how could I create an impactful program on such a diverse topic. So, the first thing I did was to break down the topic into the three critical pieces of information that the audience would need to know to be more effective at measuring work. That structure made it much easier to formulate the workshop.*

Develop Compelling Support for each Point

The second major key to a successful Three-Point talk is to offer your audience some support to back up your three key points. Real-life examples, statistics, expert opinions, and other support material can add additional credibility to your message.

The personal stories that we have talked about in the last several chapters are excellent real-life examples that can be quite compelling. Everyone loves a story.

Statistics can also be effective, but be careful. Dale Carnegie, in his book *The Quick and Easy Way to Effective Speaking*, said, "Statistics of themselves are boring. They should be judiciously used and should be clothed in language that makes them vivid and graphic." (Demonstration) *For example, if your statistics showed that your manufacturing machinery has a 20% downtime, you might make the statistic more vivid by saying, "If I were to walk out of my office ten times per day to visit the floor, two of those ten time, I would find the machinery idle."*

The testimony of an expert can also add a great deal of deal of credibility to your message. According to Cordell & Cordell, PC, "as many as 50% of all court cases utilize an expert in some capacity. Furthermore, surveys of judges have demonstrated that judges regard expert testimony as very influential in their ultimate decision, particularly where the court appoints the expert." If this type of support can influence a judge, it might be a great way to influence the people we are speaking to as well.

Summarize

Finally, to ensure that our main points are remembered, it might be a good idea to end with a summary. The best and easiest way to end a three-point talk is to just list the three key points one more time to refresh the memory of your audience.

So in summary, the three main steps to giving a great talk to inform are first, to...

1. Limit your topic to three main points
2. Develop compelling support for each topic, and
3. Summarize your main points in conclusion.

Notice how adding just a few additional impact items such as analogies, demonstrations, and examples can really clarify your information?

ACTION ITEM

Add additional support to the presentation outline you created at the end of Chapter 7 by using stories, examples, analogies, or demonstrations as your compelling support.

Topic: _____

    Point #1: _____
    (Use at least one story, example, analogy or demonstration below.)
    Compelling Support A: _____

    Compelling Support B: _____

    Compelling Support C: _____

    Point #2: _____
    (Use at least one story, example, analogy or demonstration below.)
    Compelling Support A: _____

    Compelling Support B: _____

    Compelling Support C: _____

Point #3: _____

    (Use at least one story, example, analogy or demonstration below.)

    Compelling Support A: _____

    Compelling Support B: _____

    Compelling Support C: _____

9. Impromptu Speaking

Before we jump into impromptu speaking, let's review a few of the things we have covered that help us create more impactful prepared talks.

- Enthusiasm is a secret to great presentations
- Limit talks to a minimum number of points
- Stories build rapport and help us relate to our audience
- If our purpose is to persuade, then the IAB formula can be helpful
- If our purpose is to inform, then a Three-Point Talk may be helpful
- Support for our main points builds credibility

If these things are important for us in prepared talks, doesn't it stand to reason that they would also help us in impromptu situations as well?

Of course, the major difference between prepared talks and impromptu talks is that in impromptu situations, we are likely to put additional pressure on ourselves. However, if we understand how our minds work, and use that knowledge to our advantage, with practice, we can be as comfortable—even more comfortable—in impromptu situations as we are when we deliver prepared talks.

The human brain is an incredible machine that works tremendously well under pressure. If you ask yourself questions, your brains is wonderful at providing answers. The brain works like a computer, in that the output that you get from it depends primarily on the input that you give. So if you ask general questions, you get general answers. If you ask specific questions, you get very specific answers.

For instance, if someone asks you how you are doing (a very general question,) you'll probably respond with something general like, "I'm fine," or "Great." But if someone asks, "What new tricks is the baby doing?," you are likely to give a much more detailed and specific answer.

So when you are asked to speak in an impromptu situation, the questions that you ask yourself are very important. If you're in a staff meeting and are asked, "How's your project coming?," your initial reaction may be of panic because your mind is searching through thousands of pieces of data to find an appropriate answer. But if, before you answer, you ask yourself more specific questions, you can relieve some of the pressure you have put on yourself. You are also much more likely to come up with a more specific answer.

Impromptu Talks to Inform

If the main purpose of your impromptu talk is to inform your audience, then initially, you might want to quickly organize a three-point talk outline. You might ask yourself, "What are the three most important pieces of information that this audience needs to know about this topic?" In a matter of seconds, your mind will organize three main points for you. The more you practice this technique, the faster and easier the answers will come to you. So, if you have trouble in the beginning, realize that it will get easier.

After you have the three main points, ask additional questions to yourself about each specific point. "How is the budget?" "How are we on the proposed schedule?" "How happy is the client?"

This sounds like a lot of work, but in reality, your brain will process this information very, very quickly. And it is also okay to work through this process somewhat out loud. As you are thinking, you might say something like, "As far as the project goes, the three main things we are dealing with are..."

Impromptu Talks to Persuade

If the main purpose of your impromptu talk is to persuade, then you may want to quickly organize an IAB (Incident-Action-Benefit) talk. Again, stories are a powerful way to persuade people. All you have to do is make it easy for your brain to access an appropriate story or incident for the topic you are speaking on.

The following words work like magic:

"That reminds me of the time..."

That simple phrase accesses the part of your subconscious mind that stores memories. When you say that phrase (either verbally or silently,) your subconscious mind begins to search for a specific incident related to the topic. Of course the Action part of the IAB formula is just a concise sentence stating what you are trying to persuade your audience to do. The Benefit is the benefit that your audience will receive if they take your advice.

Let's practice so you can see how easy this process is. See how fast you can come up with an impromptu talk on "Driving Safely." Verbally say the words, "That reminds me of the time..." Pause your reading and try to prepare a talk on this topic.

It may have taken you a second or two to come up with an appropriate incident, but the process you went through was probably something like this. If you had trouble coming up with a topic immediately, you probably narrowed down the topic to something more specific. Instead of "Driving Safely," you may have thought of an incident related to wearing seatbelts, regularly checking safety equipment, drinking and driving, or something else related to the topic. Once you decided on a more specific topic, the incident probably came pretty quickly.

As you relay the incident to your audience, be thinking about the Action/Benefit you want to end with. The more powerful the Action/Benefit, the more likely you are to win your audience to your way of thinking.

Bridging

What happens if the topic you are asked to speak on goes against your beliefs or is outside of your experience. You may have to use a technique called bridging. Bridging is a technique in which you change the topic slightly to fit the point that you really want to make to your audience.

The bridging technique might sound something like this, "There may be others on the panel (or within my company, or that I work with) who have more experience in this subject, but I think the real key to what you are asking is _____, and that reminds me of the time…"

All we are doing here is creating a foundation for a talk that we can deliver expertly and with confidence. We may be responding to a situation in which someone is trying to put us on the defensive, and using this technique will allow us to be more in control of the situation. It is a more proactive approach. This technique is especially helpful in question and answer sessions, and Chapter 10 will go into even more detail.

ACTION ITEM

Before your next meeting or presentation, think about possible questions that might be asked of you. For each possible question, determine if the purpose of the answer you give would be to inform the questioner or audience or to persuade the questioner or audience.

Design a response for each possible question using either the IAB formula to persuade or the Three-Point format to inform.

By doing this exercise, the odds of an audience member throwing you off your game with an impromptu question is very low.

10. Question and Answer Periods

One of the most challenging types of impromptu speaking situations can be question and answer periods, but these situations are also places where we as speakers can really shine and gain tremendous credibility with our audience. If we have used the processes and techniques from this book to establish solid trust and rapport with our audience, then the question and answer periods at the end of our talk will usually be fairly cordial and actually easy.

Quick Tips

There are a few simple things we can do to insure that we remain in control during question and answer sessions as well as stave off negative questions. Below are just a few simple tips to help.

1. **Limit the time for Questions.** Keep the time period short. Two or three minutes is usually plenty of time to field a few questions. It is best to announce the amount of time you are offering just after your talk is concluded and just before you take the first question. You might say something like, "I believe we have two minutes remaining for questions. Who has the first question?"

2. **Specifically ask for a Single Question.** Rather than asking for questions in a general way such as,

"Any questions?" or "Does anybody have a question about this topic?" you might ask more specific questions to get your audience to respond more quickly. Even, "Who has the first question?" will get you a better response. Many times, people will be intimidated about asking the first question, so you may have to "prime the pump" with something like, "A question I'm often asked is..." and then answer the question as if someone from the audience had asked the question. Many times, audience members may be too nervous to be the first to ask a question, but they will be more than happy to jump in and ask the second question. This little trick lets them off the hook.

3. **Raise your Hand.** As you ask for questions, raise your hand above your head. This gets the audiences attention, and often, certain members of the audience will raise their hand immediately. This little tip may help us avoid a long pause before the first question is asked.

4. **Repeat the Question for the Audience.** The bigger the room is, the less likely that everyone in the audience will have heard the entire question that was asked, so it is a good idea to repeat the question. This activity does two things. First, by repeating the question, especially when you are using a microphone, you let the entire audience hear the question (this is vital when recording your talk

to tape by the way.) Second, you give yourself a few seconds to think of a response.

5. **After a Question or Two, ask for a Final Question.** A great way to do this is to say something like, "I have time for one final question. Who has the final question?" Make sure and stay within the time frame of the initial time period you gave the audience for questions. The key is to have audience members still willing to ask additional questions at the end of the stated time period. Chances are, the will seek you out after the meeting. Nothing will increase the confidence of a speaker more than having a group of people searching the speaker out at the end of a talk just to get additional information.

Adversarial Questions

From time to time, you may come across someone in your audience who will either purposefully try to trip you up or who may just be having a bad day and inadvertently takes it out on you. In these situations, we have to always remember that we are in control of the speech or talk, and no one can embarrass us unless we relinquish some of that control.

Human reaction is to respond in kind to threatening or adversarial behavior from others, but in public speaking, a negative reaction can practically eliminate the trust and rapport that we spent the entire presentation building. So step one is to stay calm and look for opportunities to create a more positive outcome.

If the question asked is truly something that would be either inappropriate to respond to or might cause you or your company embarrassment, one of the first things you can do is change the question. Really. Just because someone asks us a question a certain way does not mean that we have to answer the exact question that was asked. As we repeat the question back, we can alter the question somewhat (not entirely, but somewhat,) to an easier question to answer. If necessary, a bridge can also be useful (See Impromptu Speaking, Chapter 9.)

Here's an example.

"I heard a rumor that your CEO is being investigated for tax fraud. Have an formal charges been filed yet?"

If you answered that question, "Yes," then you have confirmed the rumor. If you answer the question "No," you have also opened up a can of worms. All the follow-up questions from that point are going to be about the rumor.

A different way to respond would be to say, "The gentleman was asking about rumors of corporate scandal, and I have to admit that I'm not the most active participant around the water cooler. But that does remind me of a conversation that I had with a client recently in which he went out of his way to tell me how happy he was with the work, the integrity of our executives, and the friendliness of our staff."

A good tip to use in conjunction with this approach is that when you repeat the question, look at other members of the audience, and then answer the question to other members of the audience as well. If you make eye contact again with the person who asked the question before another question is asked, chances are, the person with ask a follow up. After the next question is asked, though, he will lose interest.

Q&A to Sell

On many occasions, as you become better and better as a speaker, civic and trade associations as well as chambers of commerce may ask you to speak to a group. One of the quickest ways to insure that you are not asked to speak again is to overtly sell your product or service during the presentation. However, the question and answer session is a great time to promote yourself.

As you begin to wrap up your answer, you may add a little plug for yourself like, "In fact, that is what many of our current clients had also been looking for, and we were able to help them. I'd be happy to talk with you after the program if you'd like to hear more." Other members of the audience who had similar questions might come see you at the end of the presentation as well.

Remember that Q&A sessions are just another opportunity for us to speak in an impromptu situation, so the same rules apply. Stories build trust and rapport, enthusiasm overcomes all faults, if we are trying to inform then we need to keep our points concise, and if we need to persuade our audience then the Incident-Action-Benefit formula will work superbly.

11. Final Thoughts

One of the most important things to remember about public speaking is that you may never totally eliminate all of your nervousness, but 51% is a winning majority. Your mind is a fantastic computer with an unlimited hard-drive that retains all your past successes, failures, and perceived failures. But the mind tends to focus on the memories that are the most painful. So, as you speak, your mind may play video tapes and recordings from the past. If all you give your mind to focus on are situation in which you have perceived that you have failed, then as that video tape plays in your head, the nervousness will increase.

The only way to change the tapes in our mind from negative experiences to positive experiences is create more and more positive experiences that crowd out the negative. As those positive experiences—those successes in front of people—grow and grow, the nervousness and anxiety will diminish.

One of the fastest ways to increase your confidence in front of a group is to get a good coach. Someone who will point out the things you are doing right, not the minor things you may be doing wrong. We get more of what we reinforce, so if we focus on the minor negatives, we will get more of them. If you count "Uhms" you will find that over time, your "Uhms" will increase. But if you focus on the positives—

enthusiasm, clarity, conciseness, confidence—you'll get more of those things as well. By the way, when we focus on the positive things that we are doing right when we speak, as a side-benefit, the "Uhms" will diminish significantly.

In my experience, professional speakers with fruit on the tree (many successes in front of groups,) tend to be the best coaches. One of the best ways to choose a coach is to see him or her in action. Is the speaker approachable and likable? Is he or she able to create a confident presence in front of the group? Is there trust between the speaker and audience? And does the feedback that I get from the coach increase my confidence or diminish it? These are all questions that should be asked before choosing a coach.

The **Fearless Presentations** program offered by The Leader's Institute is a fantastic way to apply all of the tips and techniques that are talked about in this book under the direction of a positive speaking coach. This two-day program takes participants through a step-by-step process to help them create, organize, and deliver confident, polished presentations. This program is offered in various locations all over the United States on a public basis throughout the year, and private classes can be organized with just a few participants. This program can also be tailored to the needs of your group.

In fact, in my ten years as a speaking coach, I've never seen a faster or easier way to become a confident speaker than with Fearless Presentations. You'll see your confidence grow literally overnight. You can find information about this program at www.leadersinstitute.com or call toll-free at 1-800-872-7830.

Another of our programs that has helped thousands of people overcome self-consciousness and nervousness in front of groups is **High Impact Leaders**. This program meets in four half-day sessions, and helps participants become more confident in informal speaking situations such as leading or participating in meetings. This program also focuses in other areas of leadership such as gaining cooperation, resolving conflicts, and influencing people.

Bottom-line return on investment from this program is increased dramatically (by as much as 300%) when teams from the same company attend this program together. This program can also be tailored to fit the needs of your group. You can also find information about this program at www.leadersinstitute.com or call toll-free at 1-800-872-7830.

Whether you use our programs or find a coach of your own, remember that the more success that you create in public speaking situations, the more confident you will become. You may never eliminate all the butterflies in your stomach, but with a little practice and some good coaching, you may be able to get those butterflies to fly in formation.

Good luck to you.   And if you have any specific questions about public speaking or if you would like me to work with you on designing visuals, you are welcome to e-mail me at doug@leadersinstitute.com or call me toll free at 1-800-872-7830 x100.